...open the book
find them all!

Contents

The racerunner is the fastest lizard in the world...

There are over 6,500 types of reptiles found in the world. The longest is the reticulated python. The tiniest is the dwarf gecko, and the heaviest is the saltwater crocodile.

...it can run faster than most people.

I know what a reptile is!

lizard

snake

tortoise

Reptiles have lived on our Earth
for over 300 million years.

Reptiles have **scaly** skin. They can live in water or on land. They include slithering **snakes** and huge crocodiles. So what else is there to know?

crocodile

All reptiles have scaly skin

The world of reptiles

What do reptiles have in common?
What makes them **different** from
other animals?

They lay eggs

All reptiles lay eggs.
When these hatch the
babies look like mini
versions of their parents.

Reptile eggs are soft

They shed skin

Reptiles have scaly skin, which gets worn
out. They shed their skin from time to
time leaving the fresh one underneath.

They are very old

Reptiles have lived on our Earth for a very
long time. Pterosaurs were huge flying
reptiles that lived with the dinosaurs.

Tree snakes

Snakes have long **bendy** bodies that wriggle along. They live all over the world.

The horned viper lives in the hot desert. It wriggles across the sand in an "s" shape.

python

Snakes can bend around branches

Sand snakes

Some snakes are very good at living in trees – they can coil their bodies around branches.

Some snakes are as small as pencils.

horned viper

I'm a rat snake

forked tongue

crush

2
It then crushes the egg using the muscles in its body.

3
It sucks out the inside then spits out the squashed shell.

Snake snacks

Snakes eat any animals they can catch, from tiny insects to animals as big as a deer. This egg-eating snake has a super-stretchy mouth – it can swallow an egg twice the size of its head!

stretch

spit

1
The snake unhooks its jaws and swallows the enormous egg.

fangs!

Some snakes have big teeth called fangs.

The snake has a long tongue called a forked tongue. This has two points at the end.

Snakes taste and smell using their tongues. They flick them out to "taste" the air.

9

Snake attack!

Most snakes are quite harmless but a few are very **dangerous** indeed.

a hungry anaconda

The cobra has a very dangerous bite. It rears up and stretches out its neck, then it strikes with its poisonous fangs.

Fangs

Vipers have two teeth, called fangs, which are filled with poison. They bite animals, injecting them with poison. Then they eat them.

Vipers can fold
their fangs whe

Tortoises...

Tortoises are easy to spot – they have their **homes** on their backs.

Under the shell

sleepy

When a tortoise is scared or tired, it pulls its head and legs under its shell.

I walk very slowly

12 Tortoises live longer than any other animal. The oldest we know of lived for 150 years.

...and Turtles

Turtles are like tortoises but they live in **water**. They can breathe in water and on land.

My legs are like fins

Baby dash

Sea turtles bury their eggs on beaches under the sand. The babies have to dig their way out and race to the sea.

Snap!

The alligator snapping turtle has a pink bit on its tongue that it wriggles in the water. Fish think it's a worm and swim over. SNAP! The turtle gobbles them up.

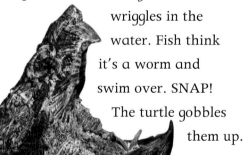

The alligator snapping turtle has one of the most powerful bites of any animal.

13

Sticky fingers

Gecko grip

This gecko has special toes that are covered in tiny hairs. These hairs help the gecko grip any surface – so it can run up walls and walk upside down.

I'm the smallest

The smallest lizard in the world is a tiny gecko found in the Caribbean. It is small enough to fit on an American quarter coin.

Run!

Lizards are very good at getting from place to place. Many can run very fast and some can climb up walls and across ceilings.

Flying lizards

Lizards can't fly but a few have special skin that they stretch out like a parachute, allowing them to glide from tree to tree.

14

Lizards

Most lizards have long bodies, thin tails, and four legs with toes at the ends for **gripping** things.

Giant dragons

The Komodo dragon is the biggest lizard in the world. It's as long as a small car.

Komodo dragons can swim and climb trees.

Chameleons

Lizards love to eat insects. This chameleon quickly flicks out its incredibly long, sticky tongue to catch flying insects.

I spy an eye

A good grip

The chameleon is very good at climbing trees. Its toes can stretch out wide to grip onto twigs and branches.

Curly tails

Chameleons have special tails that can curl around branches of trees to help them climb.

This gila monster is one of only two poisonous lizards.

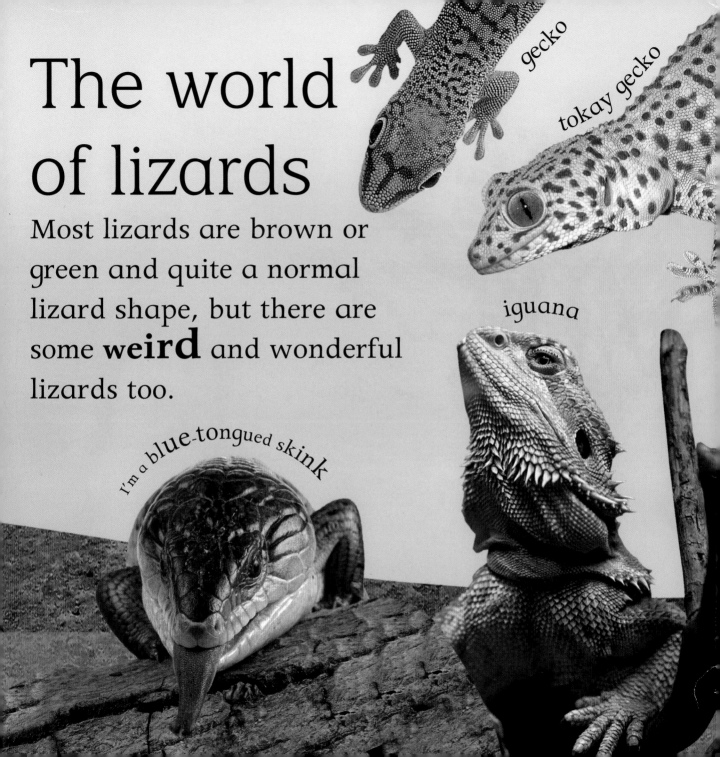

The world of lizards

Most lizards are brown or green and quite a normal lizard shape, but there are some **weird** and wonderful lizards too.

gecko

tokay gecko

iguana

I'm a blue-tongued skink

Reptile giants

Lurking underwater are the **giants** of the reptile world. Meet the fearsome crocodiles, alligators, and their relatives, the gharials.

WOW! This is how **BIG** a fully grown crocodile looks. That's huge!

zzZZZ

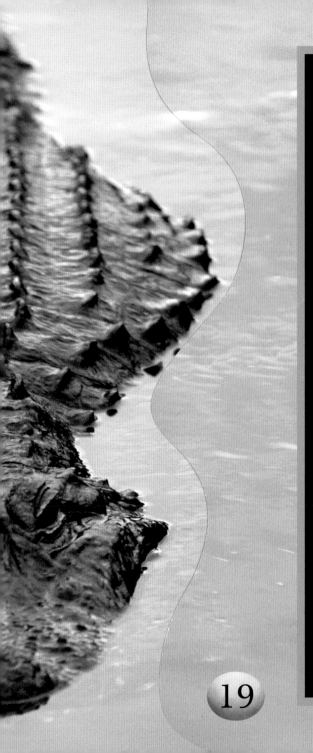

Proud parents

Many reptiles lay their eggs then leave their babies to look after themselves. The mother crocodile, however, lays her eggs and guards them fiercely. When they hatch she pops the babies into her mouth to keep them safe.

Baby crocodiles start their lives at about the length of a pencil and can grow to as long as a minibus!

19

LONDON, NEW YORK,
MELBOURNE, MUNICH, and DELHI

Written by
Penelope Arlon

Designed by
Sonia Moore and Sophie Pelham

Jacket designer Natalie Godwin
Production editor Sean Daly
Production Claire Pearson
Publishing manager Bridget Giles
Art director Rachael Foster

First published in Great Britain in 2008 by
Dorling Kindersley Limited
80 Strand, London, WC2R 0RL

A CIP catalogue record for this book is available
from the British Library.

ISBN: **978-1-40533-211-8**

Colour reproduction by Media Development and
Printing, United Kingdom

Printed and bound in China by
Hung Hing off-set Printing Co., Ltd

Discover more at
www.dk.com